GUARDIAN

GUARDIAN

Poems by
Cleopatra Mathis

THE SHEEP MEADOW PRESS
Riverdale-on-Hudson • New York

All inquiries and permission requests should be addressed to:
The Sheep Meadow Press, Post Office Box 1345,
Riverdale-on-Hudson, New York 10471.

Designed and Typeset by the Sheep Meadow Press.
Distributed by the Sheep Meadow Press.

Printed on acid-free paper in the United States. This book meets the guidelines for permanence and durability of the Committee on Production Guidelines for Book Longevity of the Council on Library Resources.

Library of Congress Cataloging-in-Publication Data:

Mathis, Cleopatra, 1947–
        Guardian : poems / by Cleopatra Mathis
            p.   cm.
        ISBN 1-878818-58-9 (alk . paper)
    I. Title.
    PS3563.A8363G83   1995
    811'.54—dc20   95-39158
                                                        CIP

The Sheep Meadow Press gratefully acknowledges grants from the National Endowment for the Arts and the New York State Council on the Arts, which helped in the publication of this book.

ACKNOWLEDGMENTS

Thanks to the editors of the following journals, where many of these poems first appeared:

Agni Review, Caprice, Greenfield Review, Kenyon Review, New Virginia Review, Ohio Review, Pivot, Ploughshares, Puerto del Sol, and *The Seneca Review.*

"The Small Matters of the Everyday" first appeared in the anthology *After the Storm.*

Section 10 of "Exile" first appeared as "Eve Speaks" in *Cape Discovery: The Fine Arts Work Center Anthology.*

"Seven Months" first appeared in the anthology *First Light.*

"The Guardian" (published as "Like Angels") first appeared in the anthology *Winged Spirits.*

I would like to gratefully acknowledge Scott Momaday's *House Made of Dawn,* to which my poem "Sons" is indebted, and the etchings of William Blake, which were the inspiration for the poems in "Exile." My thanks to Kathy Harp for her computer expertise. And to Pamela Harrison, Kristel Heinemann, Stanley Kunitz, Stanley Moss, and Bill Phillips, my deepest gratitude for their encouragement and support.

"Poem for Marriage" is for Elizabeth Awalt.
"The Story" is for David Roberts, M.D.

CONTENTS

II.   THE ART OF EXILE

For Martha Webster

I

GUARDIAN

POEM FOR MARRIAGE

Pretend you have never been in love,
pretend that nothing has changed you,
that it is possible to live without violation.
You could go back to the girl you were
at fifteen, reading for hours in a kind of sleep,
angry to be awakened—the lives around you
never the emotional equal of those
you lived on the page. Those years
belonged to a loneliness you never questioned;
so complete, the sweet ache of the self
gazed back at you from the mirror
as if she were the stranger. Now if you wake alone,
it's only because the other is still sleeping.
At the edge of the Atlantic, you rise
in slow motion, needing to leave it all
undisturbed: the mutual plans and concerns,
the temporary obliteration of sex.
Exhilarated by the privacy and the light, you walk out
to the beach, and watching the tide play
its trick of distance, decide to go
to the land's farthest reach, that ghostly point
where the water's body joins the sky.
You walk fast and straight out, through shallow pools
becoming more frequent and deep until you sink
sometimes to the knee. Until there's more
empty water than sand and it is so clean
that nothing speaks of living; even the one
sea-rotted body of a man o' war is no more
than a marker your eye uses to keep perspective
on what's large, what's small. Looking back,
you can barely see the toy-sized house,
white on white in the haze: it has nothing
to do with you. Everything out here
has the holy cast of blue, everything is filled
with wind. And finally, the sand's last edge—
the entire ocean looms. How easy,
you think, to take one more step;
to walk until your legs flail and go useless,

your body washing forward, over and under
with its involuntary struggle, and you turn
from the confines of breath to a world
wholly imagined . . . But love
has had its way with you; that tide pulls you back
to its fragmentary shore of loss and gain.
Until you are not yourself but part
of another story, as if your life were a child
crying for milk.

BLUES: LATE AUGUST

Bluefish boil the water silver; they tangle in the chase
and the frantic smelt run headlong onto the sand,
caught by the blinding mirror, the water's

skimming sheet. And in the tide's remove, the knife-like
bodies hardly struggle, laid out in one long row
like silverware by a child's hand. All the bathers

scramble out of the sea, fearful of the indiscriminate
bluefish jaws, and around our heads, the gulls
flail about, sharp-eyed and diving, a frenzy

guarding the feast. All along, the ocean
turns its back to the spectacle, locked
in its usual resolve, but I can't move

for love of the world, its terror and sufficiency.

WHO KNOWS

where his tumor came from?
My husband wants to bury it
in the food we eat: wine or no wine,
what does it drink? The mysterious X and Y
of coupling and conception
swelled their way to pregnancies—
his headache, my nausea,
CAT scan, ultrasound,
our diagnoses. Can we trust
meditation and massage, the surgeon's
knife, the itch and burn
of stitches, or the work of scars?
Oh the products of our labor:
one in a jar
left on a shelf for study,
the other we take home
in blue blankets. And what is it
that takes hold in the baby's
dream and brings him back, the long
siren cry of a baby fighting sleep?
Lower and lower he wails,
falling into dark, a rondo
slowing only to rise. What will satisfy
the little master? He pulls
at the unlikely breast, bluish drops
gleaming in his mouth, slack now;
finished in the crook of my arm,
the head lolls. Nothing else
can get milk out; my furious pumping
makes a poor ounce.
But how the baby fattens, little pear
thighs and such knees, such round
ineffectual feet. Maybe they make tumors too.
For that matter, what about the plum's
decaying fruit against the screen,
the seeds at the heart
of the tree's last apples,
vivid as pain in the appetite of snow—

white fists of too-early,
disfiguring snow.
Toppling in his fat suit
the eight-month-old gurgles.
Does all the dumb world know?
Maybe anything the shape of a head
knows, or any one of the body's eyes
where heaven-knows-what can get in.
Oh splinter, speck of affliction,
from where? Tiny, tiny, the god cell
wants to make brothers.
If you listen, it howls, ordinary life
with its quantum leap.
We turn in our beds, we turn and turn.

HOME BABIES: NEWBORN AND TUMOR

This one won't throb, just twitches
in his sleep. Cells split, programmed
to lengthen the fingers, straighten the arm.
He's made one black diaper full,
one ambiguous smile. He doesn't know he smiles.
In forty-eight hours, just once
has he clearly opened his eyes: the surgeon's razor
on a quarter inch of debatable skin.
They say he's yellow: give him light, oil
the blackening knot on the belly.
What instinct for the domestic—
his little fist, little scream!

The other is a born architect
with too many plans. He won't stop
buzzing, he pounds and pounds.
He wants to crack daddy's head, he wants
to leap from his own heaven,
he wants to be God!
Dig, dig the traitor out.
Find the blueprint; cut and scrape
the throbbing molecules, octopi,
fastidious structure invading the house.
Under lights, daddy's face shines
large in the great pain, white
in the theatre of unsweet sleep.
Around him, the surgeons close their circle,
trapping the invader
laced into the artery's midline,
foundation for the head and spine.
They sigh and meditate. Vivaldi, wakemi, sushimi,
ya ya ya. One hand proffers the tiny knife.
What can deliver this fakir?

THE STORY

Innocent and earnest, good at marathons, the surgeon
believed in his hands; he said
he'd cut the tumor out, a convoluted unnatural thing
wrapping its tentacles around the brain's little house.
Nothing more than architecture, then he paused:
he knew about the maze, the puzzle.
He put on his white clothes; over his entire being
he laid white cloth. He gathered his men
and the one woman, and they all went in
with sharp instruments. The drill took the bone
and the red spray flew. They found the right room
in the back of the head. They found the tiny monster heart
wavering near the brain stem.
But no microscope could turn down the folds
of the pineal gland, where the soul looked out
its infinite window and saw the altered light.
Saw the giant hand that was not God's.
No scalding oil fell; the soul did not shiver
and hide its face. The light of science
went on burning, and so did the knife,
dismantling cell by cell. But the soul was calm.
It waited out the industrious nine-hour sleep,
dozing itself at times to avoid the blinding
overhead lamp. The soul sang its little songs,
dreamless infant songs: far beneath and years gone,
complementary to the Mozart the surgeon played.
Humming away, the soul wove a tuneless cover
for every memory of intrusion, fear, and pain.

And when you woke—
cut even where the clamps had held the mask to your face,
bandaged and swollen and clean,
changed but for the wide pacific blue of your eyes—
love still lay there: handsome, without innocence,
and utterly faithful.

AFTER SURGERY

What is this circle they've carved
in the back of your skull? O pumpkin,
blank face, a great reposing head
waiting in your autumn bed.
We light a candle, post a vigil
—but too late: pain has made its harvest.
You with the taste of ash in your mouth,
not sleeping.

        Little earth, how solid you are,
even after the knife. And your eyes,
deep moons. How long can you lie there
with the will to watch
the tangled night, the mountain
over you, the god of iron?

AFTER THE OPERATION

1.

He cannot name the specifics of his pain.
Hurt, he says, *I hurt*. He is a child
growing younger every moment
his eyes meet mine. This is language
before language; this is sound the infant knows,
muffled, ordinary, the merge of pure sensation.
All the senses make one great noise, a storm
abiding in his head. A monster stitch
snakes its way up from the base of his neck.
It stings, it aches. They've taken away
part of the bone, a circle
carved in the back of his skull.
It makes him tilt his head, walk sideways,
makes him vomit the milk and bread.
A lump rises along the scar,
resembling the swell of wind against a sail.
Inside him, the fluid
give and take of pressure
pushes against containment,
a disturbed water. Sobbing and sobbing,
the infant rush and heave in a body
that is no longer self but matter.
After forty years, he is again all possibility.
What is that life inside,
what's growing? The tide force
heaves toward birth, the incoherent
speech falling useless on the sand.

2.

Months pass. Hair begins to cover the scar,
fine strands, like a kind of weed we've seen
washed up on broken land after the sea's
weather. Little by little,
the tide turns; he forgets
exactly what it meant—that invasion

of heat and light in the privacy of his mind.
Only the ghost word, pain
with its abstract terror,
remains. He vacations at the sea,
and how he loves this, the restored
cold on the beach, the water
escaping the form imposed by snow and ice
sculpting the fifty or so feet of khaki sand:
The waves themselves are less
visible in the water's mass, and full of white.
They are the color of the spirit,
which does not inhabit,
no, not one particle of the stony, fragile shore.

BABY ODE

Here's my praise
in the name of skin on skin, that magic
wherever. A bottle of wine,
midnight kisses, and the baby begins.
Months before she shows, before you'll marvel
at her belly's shine, its inverted button
and solid lump, sign of the life
whose random thrust is the riddle
against your hand, the riddle of sex and name.
When she no longer walks but waddles,
an ever-ballooning shape
hungry for honey cake and women, the impossible
shower of tiny blue, tiny pink,
there's labor and your part:
to take the flack and understand
the monitor of the invisible heart;
to guide her breath, the panting
to relieve her panic; no free moment
to call the in-laws betting quarters at home.
Labor grows and when you think
she'll break, you'll break
in the white hours from dusk to dawn,
every fear comes true in her quick fever,
an infection they guard with a sterile sheet
and her tied-down hands. Now, says the doctor,
and the word rings across your universe;
rings with the wet slap of flesh
against her stomach. One moment of *now*
as the fish comes to land.
Then the thin song, the glimpse of flesh
you catch through bloody mucus,
this bit of protoplasm with the jerking
tiny fist. *Like* is all you think:
this is like . . . but the birth itself
is already escaping—
no analogy belongs, no word
comes to rest. The blue mass
goes rosy, the afterbirth descends.

They offer the scissors
to cut the cord, to force the knot
you'll see blacken and fall away.
Half in a faint, you watch
the needle that sews her together again,
the needle that opens the vein in his foot.
And in hardly an hour, a wonder
more like geometry: the first blind suck
completes a triangle, head turned
in the only direction the baby knows.
A small animal dumb in the forest,
he is true to the path, a determined
physicality, like the body's first release:
the diaper's one load of black
meconium, a package of waste
from the nine-months' water and salt.

Now baby is a pure thing
smelling of corn flour and air
and sweet mustard shit. Even the clean sign
of circumcision you'd rather not think of
finishes the tip of his body's
otherwise seamless skin.
Nighttime is a circle, the baby's
two-hour kamikaze of cry and sleep.
When you think you'll never sleep again,
then seven blessed hours and the panicky
silence when you open your eyes.
Stumbling to cribside, you hold your palm
over the moth-like give and take of air.
So the days pass: over and over
you test his breath and measure his body.
You wash his soft clothes, you scrub
the yellow spit-up from your shirt.
Ah, you say ah, fingering the swollen gums
for the one pearly tooth. Before you know,
it's mashed chicken and peas,
stink out the pants leg, the rhyme and candle

of the birthday song. The drum of the wall
as he bangs the crib, the dragging blanket,
and the bottle, thrown.

APOLOGY

He loves her, he loves the child
lying between them, though its presence
denies them access to each other.
Too easy to lose that small cusp of a body
in the tangle of sheets. Gingerly he reaches
across, grazing the flannel
of the thick gown, the nursing bra
which guards the unfamiliar breasts.
A few pats is what he manages,
the briefest intersection.
Heavy it weighs, this frailty,
this triangle the baby makes
of their love. Everything he has cared for
moves in a straight line to the physical
breach the baby has become,
fulcrum to his desire. And as her body
removes to another point in time,
her mind weighs only the external—
where he is, what he says, how much
attention he pays to the soggy diaper.
Unlikely extension of their cupidity,
nine months of lambent fear, the labor,
the healthy child,
whose good luck was all they wished,
is precisely how she triples their equation:
more of him is what she wants, and seeing him
helpless in response, does not know
how to forgive.

SEVEN MONTHS

A slight infection of the ear,
then plain cold human will:
his whole body said no.
He stiffened in her arms, screamed
to see the nipple bared.
After two days of pumped milk and tears,
screamed even at the great white bra
when she unbuttoned her blouse.
Midnight came, and when he stirred
she sang, coaxed the baby
close, then as he fell to sleep,
tricked him with the gradual
transfer from bottle to body.
He shuddered, his lips moved
half-opened on her skin and he took back
the hard, veined breast
swollen as big as his head.
Pain was part of it; she ached
with relief as his clean taut pull
drew the arrows from her chest.
She settled back in the rocker—
dim pinpoints of stars, moths
tapping the screen. Ordinary September.
But the little mouth was resolute:
last time, last time
went the rhythm of its suck.
What could she do
but give him up.

STAR CHILD

Blessed visitor, he hasn't made a home yet.
His ceiling imitates the heavens, his door
withholds a universe of household sounds.
Attracted, repelled, he drifts
in his crib, and I lean into the planetary light
to pull him in. Outside language,
he points the way, directing me to say
each name in the constellation of his room.
The compass of his finger is my guide.
It turns till I go hoarse or dizzy or mistake
what he wants, naming the wrong shape.
His whole body trembles at my error:
rage is his one clear vowel.
Lost in the cluttered world,
what comfort in *sun, moon, cloud*:
those bodies I've pasted on his blue-papered wall?
He sobs until we abandon all
syllables for kisses. And clings, offering earth
the name that makes me famous: his easy
automatic *Mama*. He puts his hand in my mouth.

THE BABY WALKED

I didn't want to see
his first haphazard step.
I would not see him walk and went on

digging the track of the brittle root.
Bindweed had taken the garden,
vines so thick I couldn't unravel them

without breaking my flowers' simple necks.
Above the winding heart-leafed wires
starred cups of campanula

filled with bees. Behind me
the baby struggled to stand.
The baby fell and rose and fell.

The baby was gold, his eyes
a blue that painters know—his likeness
floated on the Sistine ceiling.

Silly mother, I could not touch him
without fear of disturbing his perilous beauty.
Safer to stay away, wrestling

with morning glory, innocent name of the pest
I'd planted years before. Its white root
traveled bed to bed, a long finger

reaching. Now in its profusion
a great hive hung. If I jarred the fence
even slightly, an angry buzzing

circled above the flowers. The baby in the grass
chortled, his fat thighs glistened.
He reached for anything that flew,

handfuls of grass rose with him.
Two stings pulled me back,
one as I worked to slowly, steadily

pull the taproot up whole
and with the right motion, let go.
Only to see it break again, and dig deeper,

searching for each piece as if it were the secret
of the vine's tight hold. The second sting
was meaner: the same hand

ached and swelled. I freed what stems I could,
blue stars, white stars—the baby
stumbled, caught himself, and walked.

THE PERFECT SERVICE

The truth is, the child protects you, takes away
the obligation to be someone other than yourself.
In the full-blown spring, his clumsy feet
hidden in the grass, his fat palms in the thick
clumps of narcissus, everything's naked.
The earth is full of openings: he might disappear
if you turn your back. Bees, blackflies, the endless teeming
world hovers around his flawless head.
It would go on existing—and what about you,
how could you face all this beauty in his absence?
The expectation of loss makes you crazy. Better to have
the cold, to walk out without dread in the deepening snow—
winter's breath affirming your own nature—
how firmly you fastened layer after layer on his small body.

RAPTOR

You make the mistake of telling him
about the stump just off the path to the beaver dam.
How in the canopy of hemlock, the deer's
wintering ground, a great horned owl dragged down
dove after dove, leaving on his makeshift table
mats of feathers and thrown-up stones,
the egg-shaped pellets of rib and skull.
He's got to go there, he pleads,
not happy with the three tail feathers you saved.
Death is deep in him, its pull
certain in the details of his play, the way
benign objects become guns and knives.
Let's be bad guys, his small voice quivers,
us and *them* rising out of the dark
that you think now is fundamental.
But your son's not like some other children
you've heard about, the ones who hide
from their mothers, run laughing into the road.
Victor over every monster, he would never
leave his bed in the dead of night,
unbolt the door and let himself out
into the heavy snow. He wouldn't do that,
would he? —wander, dreaming
until the cold carried him away.

MOTHER'S DAY, 1993:
HEARING WE WILL BOMB BOSNIA

You so love the child, you take away
every unsafe thing, surround him
with softness as he sleeps. You have no way,
truly, to keep him unharmed, and knowing this,
you live with a certain condition, a swelling
in the complicated region of the chest.
It catches you unaware this lovely morning
as you drink your second cup of coffee,
twenty minutes past his usual waking. You resist
what-if, reminding yourself
he hardly slept last night. You've learned
what asthma can do; you've seen his blue face
when the airways close, then for days, dull
shadows under his eyes. Called from sleep,
you've found him sitting up, both hands braced
against the wall. You hold him
tight in your arms, his thin shoulders, trunk, hips
racked with coughing, every muscle and nerve
negotiating the art of breathing. And though
you've bought the machine that like magic
opens his tubes and restores the air, sweet gulps
he takes in like a drug, and gives him back to perfect sleep,
every bizarre consequence you've ever heard
comes rushing through now like a wind in spring,
a sharp risk in the blossoming world.

No wonder you turn, horrified and hating
your cowardice, from the magazine, the cover picture
of the dead child. You can't look at it:
the shrouded head, the bloody mouth
exposed and slack, then the brief, unchildlike clothing
and below that, exposed,
as if nothing in the world were wrong,
the tender arc of the belly.
Oh that familiar part of the child, the body
a mother kisses. A nation of mothers.

THE SMALL MATTERS OF THE EVERYDAY:
TWO ACCOUNTS

1.

This is the story of a man.
This is guesswork from the papers,
from all of us who need to understand
a man we thought no different from ourselves.
For don't we all imagine
the tapping inside a void, a voice inside a voice
that makes more echo than sense?
Who knows what he heard
behind the normal weight of rain and wind.
Something pursued him from room to room
until he thought it was his own pulse
ticking away at each failure. He thought
he felt his heart skip, the maneuver
of a heart made wrong, a muscle
tightening like a fist around some fear
so essential it would strike to break free.

He's got his two kinds of music:
classical and country, one open, the other shut.
As brandy complements the former—the expansive talker
in any group—beer closes him down. Night after night,
he hunches over the bar, elbows out.
One morning he walks to work from the train,
seeing the perfect V of ducks
over the mirror and steel of buildings
and something in the accidental beauty of it
is intolerable. He thinks maybe it is his work
he hates. He's sick of the office, the politics
of his own geography; and even at 5 p.m. his partner
playing racquetball wonders at his vengeance,
at the batter and heft of his mean left hand.
He takes a physical cure, he takes three days and goes south
to hunt, crouching in the humming quiet of the blind
on a red fall morning. He looks into the marsh water
as he can no longer bear to look
at himself, or at his wife who escapes it all,

counting stitches as she knits or the minutes
for kneading bread. Her hands
are never still. He can no longer
bear to look at them, no longer bear the knife
buttering the bread, or the repeated mouths
chewing, body to feed the body; cannot bear
the truth of her body which he has filled
with bodies. Their faces surround him, and in this proof
of a future history, he sees nothing
but the futility of it all.
Who knows what stops him, what moves him
late one night to load a gun and move from room to room
taking the life of his wife and each child
sleeping, until it is time to turn the gun on himself.
But he never enters the last room
where the last child sleeps, or if he does, only looks
and leaves, or straightens covers,
or even kisses her in the way of any father
his sleeping child. She will wake to this story
and it will follow her all the days of her life.

2.

The other man, who keeps his old mother
and bathes his children, will bring out his wallet
for weapons in another country, righteous
for bombs. One goes off
in the middle of women shopping or shaking their rugs,
ordinary as weather. Spring in this soil
holds the blood's chemical trace.
Every grain of this dirt has passed through
the bones of a woman or man.

But nobody breaks terror's code, preferring to be saved
by the small matters of the everyday.
The cows chew and plod
their way over the drumlins; the children
bound for school in white stockings

wait by the lilac hedge, and the sky rains gently away
into an immaculate clearing. In the old earth,
in the silk and meal of dirt, the stalk pushes up.

A TEXT IN FORGIVENESS

In the way of all his mornings, he sits there
smoking, having risen in the pre-dawn
shifting black. Awake to nothing but the over and over
of soap and running water, he has made his way
to the kitchen, the ritual of coffee. He sits,
watching the window glass give back his own reflection,
an older man waiting. Each hour
divides room shadow from outside shadow,
until the outer light is stronger than the inner,
and with the dimming vision of himself
he is taken into day. The cold light
rises to cream and violet; he watches
the minute variations take their toll.
And when finally his hand rises, it is hard to tell
if he wants to shatter something or to beckon
a greater presence, some other body of light
opposing whatever it is behind him.

For it has become a lifetime, this waiting—
this quitting the circumstance, the predicament.
Quitting the books, their plots and voices
that all add up to one: his life as a fiction
he has made, the craft of it
outside what he really wanted.
The scene he looks out on, trees and meadow
coming clear, is resonant, exposed;
so different from the dense magnolia in his childhood yard,
a vastness and height defined only
by the limitations of beauty. The showy leaves
snapped too easily, the blossoms stood up like wax.
Never understanding that delicacy, deliberate as a white lie,
forbidden to climb the available branches,
he crawled into the vast canopied underside.
In that leaf-dark world and its dim pattern of silt and bark,
the visible tree became no more than a shape,
pruned and determined, an artful cover
for the interior. That reverie now
is what he wants: his fingers playing the surface

until the end he reaches is prayer,
intermediary between the two worlds.

And if he has risen to quit the night,
to mark the confluence of word and step
with the deep close hours he entered as if they were velvet,
as if he had buried his face in some ravishing solitude
with its reverberating *no*; then with enough
of these mornings he would forgive
the longing by which he lived.

THE FIGHTER

1.

It's the thrill of moving
too fast to think. The body's
sweet hunger drives you
like the sex you can't resist.
You're sixteen again, shaking off
reason; just the right word, a look,
and you throw it all away,
let go for the sheer give
of whatever's under you. The whole world
accelerates. Even with your back to the wall

your gut drives you, drives the fist.
After the first hit, you've forgotten
the insult, the latest failure.
The body goes on
pummeling and reaching till you've
separated from anger. All of it—
every exchange of blows, every sanctuary
of blessed pain, the kick way back there
that knocked you senseless.

Then you're back in the humdrum
fight of living, the monotony of is-this-all.
Real or imagined, something's nagging.
Don't push me, but no, the girl goes on
talking until you can't bear
her litany, her chain of no's,
that rosary of self she shoves in your face.
Your fist rains down on her,
the palm of your right hand
taking her left jaw until you are swinging
in dead air, gone into something
damaged or blind. You could be hitting
on anything; you've disappeared
into the ache of your hand
answering her words until they fall

with her, the unforgettable
beaten out of what she has to say.

2.

She's a dead ringer for her brother,
his face imposed on hers. He is the one
you think of when she speaks, his expression
in her half smile, a smirk
you've set into a kind of life mask.
The afterimage of him in her
has become the challenge
narrowed in her eyes. Go ahead, they say,
and knock me down; one more time
let's see if you can touch me.

She is going to carry you
until she thinks she has forgotten
what a quarter of a century
tries to hide. Until in pain
at forty she learns it is a part
of the synapse and motion of her left jaw.
Where the bone was jarred
and jarred again from its socket,
a clicking fights the flaw—
locked in the animal jaw, a snap
to mark every bite and hate
stored deep in the muscle.
And the mind can't touch that, can it?
The body keeps what is real.

ASH WEDNESDAY

The heart wants to be ice.
Come in, it says, to the spirit of breaking,
the hangnail, the impossible choice.
Jesus died, and you will be tested.
Oh the snow, six feet of it
waiting for a thaw. Still it falls,
sweeping the air, a whisper.
Who would not choose sleep?
But they all want something, they won't quit
asking. The husband, the children

claim you for theirs.
They can't see how tired you are,
how far you've traveled.
Once you almost killed a man. You held a knife
to his chest, and though something pulled you
back from hate, you were lost
in the weight of it. You wore it
like fat, the ache in your throat,
the cry when you run.

The snow covers every stain. The snow
saves anything that can live beneath it.
Time to lay down
your right arm, the industrious hand;
send your voice into the white interior.
Every night you lie curled on your side,
the path of your body as still as possible,
pressing an ear into the naked curve
of your shoulder, where you can feel
and even hear the terrifying surge of blood.

DOLL

She's five. Her hair is white, a nimbus
of curls. Her grin
starts on the left side of her face
and moves right. My name
was the first word she ever said,
and all our lives I'll see her at this age:
the sweet one, her fat dimpled hands
reaching for me as for a mother.
Not just the oldest child, guarding
the boundaries of our room,
fussing over her clutter, I was best at

standing my ground, chin-out.
But when she says she took the heat
for me, not the slaps but
his insisting body all her young years;
when she says she did it
to save me, I realize
who was the strong one. Who didn't crack
like the plaster head of my doll,
the one that got banged at odd times
when I wasn't around. *Dolli-mou,*
I called her, that ugly blond thing
who had lost her clothes, her wide eyes
stuck finally in the back of her head.
Year by year, a jagged line
moved over the crown and forehead,
opening as it took each of the black holes
once filled with a blue light.

SURVIVAL

Days I have waited for the amaryllis to unfold.
The thick red fist on its sturdy stalk
fills the window, where just beyond
the white world beckons. In February, light
begins its quiet return, a rich stranger
hastening over the snow's unbroken field,
and we think we have not been abandoned.

When I was young, fierce with hard reason,
I longed for a sign. But where could I look?
No clear winter defined limitation; ambiguity
marked the water and sky. The birds, after all,
never left: cardinals stained the yard red.
Beyond our house, the cattle stood:
skinny egrets pecked for hours on their backs.

I didn't care for flowers then.
In the first rainy months of the year, their odors
hung like a damp curtain over everything.
The row of camellia bushes, beaten back,
lined the porch, and those bruised white petals
hung on. I saw them, smelled them
from our living room where day-in, day-out, I refused
my stepfather's demands, paying with my body.
One night I stood over his reclined chair,
alone with the canned laughter
and his snore. He lay like a patient
sleeping, his body exposed, open for my work.
I held the kitchen knife steady over his chest.
The t.v. blared; nothing, I thought, could be so loud.

What saved me, I wonder thirty years later—
lost in the telling, the permission
I give myself, that place
signified by blame, the sin, the forgiving.

THE ANGELS

They bring in the knife, they show you
his sleeping body and the spot to strike.
They are quick as shadows crossing,
a knot of confusion. Then one of them
moves apart, separate from their dark impulse,
and claims your hand. She creates
another step, another purpose,
though for now she makes your tears
fall with frustration. She will not let you
do what your body wants; your teen-age body,
made purely of anger, wants to forget
the spirit, the flicker of self
that whispers through you at odd moments.
You do not yet know the art
of seeing and waiting, the way
to make change possible. And what is she
but the secret that bears your life forward.
Charitable toward this mess you live in,
she turns you away, and in that instant
you hear the night birds, the small clamor of their appeal
more lovely because they remain unseen.
A universe of wings is somehow at your window,
claiming a world you have never known
could be righteous. When the moment passes,
your hand, having lost its will,
moves away from his chest, and the chaos
takes over, those truculent voices
of fear. Years will pass before you can live
with their noise, before their presence
grows quiet, and you find her again, the one
who, without reason, made herself your mother,
and you listen.

LITTLE LIE

Among the people I have loved
and the lies I have told,
one lie stands. Trivial, impulsive,
almost funny, the lie
was not meant to hurt or flatter.
I gave my husband two new shirts,
telling him they were my grandmother's gift.
I went on talking, admiring
each color and cut, as she sat there
knitting in our house. The two
needed no reconciliation; neither desired
anything from the other.
It was my need, an automatic reaching
for what I still wanted from her.
Already I walked around wearing her name,
cooking her kind of food. Whatever was mine
I wanted to be hers and perhaps she felt
she had given me too much—yes,
I wanted to reciprocate. But I saw her
startle; she looked at me and looked
and took me in without a word.
Fifty years had passed since her family died
at the hands of the Turks, and five since Cyprus
took her last surviving cousins.
In one more year, my brother would not come home.
Disappearance, its own kind of lie,
lived a lifetime with her. Uncompromising
to the end, she had not given herself
to even the largest grief, so not once
did she mention my lie.
Now I am grown enough to see the violation,
to see that it lay like a body between us.
Sorry, I go on mumbling—though she is gone.
I buried her in our familiar ground.

THE GUARDIAN

1.

Every night she says she hears
an animal screaming—peacock or bobcat—
something wounded and dying to herald
the fleet of men rowing on thick water.
They've got her son's body in the boat,
cutting to some lost point in the veiled cypress.
This dream has nothing to do
with retribution, or even the murderers,
only the prayer—her litany, her rosary
and refrain—that he did not suffer.

2.

Meanwhile, members of a certain race
think to purify themselves.
The children of the hated other
are crying, muffled behind scarves
in anonymous laps on the bus
between two points of nowhere. A crack
rings out, in the domestic imagination
a kitchen sound; then the surprising
silence, and one of them is finished.
The newspaper shows another face
behind the window, forever shocked in that instant,
chosen to be the keeper of it all.
My mother clips the photo, a young man
whose life is stunned with knowing.
Why is the word that bears her life forward.
The curse of the saved
is to sleep like the dead, or not at all,
forever crossing the sorrowful water.
Every dawn brings the slow, tremulous doves.
She's awake to scatter old bread.

3.

Far north, with the certainty of one
who has moved away, I insist
he died quickly. Fifteen years now I have risen
and walked out the long pier to the harbor.
Gliding in the breaking dark,
dark bones on water, the fishing boats
begin to come in: *Little Infant, Jimmy Boy,*
Cast Your Net Wide.

PERSIMMON TREE

Here comes the season of consequence.
October, encompassing
all our tenses, assigning meaning to the rest.

Summer fell—a few weeks between all we can have
and what we will pay for it. And where
is your baby now? Call her Spring,

so obsessed she is with becoming. The budding,
the shying away from your own chest. A wind
blows between you. She wants to know

the exact meaning of mortality, daily
how much she weighs, and why
did you divorce, causing her such agony

in your careful back-and-forth. At twelve,
she has just two prevailing weathers:
embarrassment and scorn. So you discuss geography,

glacial formations, the types of rock and water.
You admire her fifty-six polished stones
glowing in the window. You get close enough

to tell her about the persimmons in the swamp,
your yearly search for what you called
October gold, claiming the light

in Louisiana's evening of ordinary
grays and browns. Just once, you picked through
the layers of fallen fruit, a bee-covered mash,

and pulled yourself up to eat from the filled branches.
You were eleven; you never found the tree again.
Later you thought you might have dreamed it—a thousand globes

from some fairy tale—a way of forgiving
the actual ground. You skip what else you know,
leaving out the day's companion, the friend

who would be dead in just one year. You don't mention
how you taunted her fear of breaking rules,
of water moccasins that sent you stumbling back

through higher, unfamiliar land. Her father
had to come find you—Patty, with her turned ankle,
damning you in the dark. No, your daughter

doesn't need your story. Already, brooding and refusal
cross each step, the road turning and the season,
which will claim its price.

LONG AFTERWARD

This dream is locked inside me
when I sit upright
in the middle of the night,
because the baby is crying and I must go.
But that was years ago—
though her sleep lives in my arms
and the tiny fist in my palm.

And wakened now
to the wreckage of quiet,
I guide myself back
as I would find my way
through the black of a room,
vague with the effort,

until I am both
myself and the dream-fierce child
I take into my bed. I lie
on my side, she curled into the hollow
sucking her fingers. And I go back
half-sleeping to what I hold on to:
the reparable self, the healing.

TOWARD SPRING

Light opens the field,
no longer pocked and rutted.
No mark where the child
led her horse in the unsettled air.
Quick, he took the little fences,
lunged on the line locked in her fist.
All afternoon, the raw hooves digging.

Better this: the sleeping white
cover of the one night's snow.
For these small hours, we turn back to beauty
without sacrifice, denying the god
wakened by desire. Why else
are the animals wild, the children
so insistent?

MARRIAGE

She likes the love-making, a curious phrase
she can't help associating
with bloodletting. Passion
determines her response, as the Puritans
desired the exalted and achieved it
by draining the body with leeches
they dug from swampy water.
Applied to the skin, each mouth
filled until it was a bloated sac,
stiffened, all animal, taking away
the animal blood which might claim
the spirit: that sweet breath
behind the beat, the stutter, the gasp.

Later, the weight of him
is unbearable. She is under a great stone
and though she contracts, tries to pull back
every cell into herself to make room
between them, some breathing space,
his body descends, settling
until it owns her. The stone that will forever
rest over her body with no more validation
than her name. She is nothing more
than a victim of some terrible calamity,
an earthquake perhaps when the walls
collapse on the unsuspecting family,
and the one left breathing must lie there
stunned with the weight of the surrounding dead.
And if his body once held the comfort
of a cave she found in darkest midnight,
now under the wall of his breath
she struggles against panic; thinking *love*,
repeating the certain word
against hopelessness—every effort
to recover the relinquished
dear self, find the germ of the spirit,
to enter it, and fly.

NOT WRITING

The world is indifferent—
who wants poetry but my own dark ego
setting words to its music.
Again it is night, the short day's end
with him, little child
banging against my brow, bruising
my lip with his hard gold head.
We are playing the mother game of rock, rock
forward and backward, till sleep
can take his quick body,
until I gaze on stillness: eyelashes and lips,
the slight transaction of breath.
My own eyes grow heavy,
heavier at the thought of my cluttered desk
in a far room. Oblivion,
is that what I want?
Not the orchestra and chorus
but the white rug, the folded wash,
the scrubbed porcelain sink.

THE GREAT QUIET

I have been dreaming about sleep,
eyes closed and snow
thick on the skylight.
And in the children's rooms
utter silence, only the sweet things
laid in their places and the brief order.
Nothing there but the practical
breath, the body governed by air.
No wonder I am called

away from my other life, the defining
self that admits nothing but the mind's
endless digging. I wake with a start,
fearing the moment
a child's breath falters and I am not there
to shake the body back

with this hand that drags over the page.
All I want is to sleep,
to rise before daybreak in the far room.
But what will you pay, the voice echoes

cold in the dream
where paper is piled against the window;
where my hair and skin have turned
to powder, and when I speak
to overtake the great quiet, to call back
my daughter, my son,
my throat is a long avenue of ice
cutting the familiar good words
at their source.

WRITING

From a black sky, light
falls over my desk. 5 a.m.
and the night is still a fact; the moon
like truthful speech
continues to throw a path.
How can I wake to follow its brief direction?
In rooms above me, a dry cough
threatens a sleeper.
The quiet waits. The breathing
of the ones I love and fight
fills the cold air.

II

THE ART OF EXILE

EXILE

1. A Creation

Let go, becoming one
drop out of sea,
which was then a body of mist
watering the whole face of the ground.
Wandering above it, the uninformed
particle, not needing. No cloud,
no fog to blanket a self.
A seed existed, unconscious,
decent; all sight and perspective,
an imagination in the whole of being.

Then God wove himself in light,
in communion with all blue space,
and closed around like a fist
which gathered up the breath of me.
I joined the wedding of elements,
the melding of salt and sand
that dragged me down
to the black bed of the sea
and held me to a shape, a pulse
to hold the pouring of his mineral.
Liquid filled me, then something
stolen, and I hardened,
accretion of shell around the grain
of who I was. I rose up like silk
out of the skein of water,
rose out of man's loss, the rib
bent into place, the contagion,
the blue arc and syllable of my doubt.

Adam opened over me—
husband, the predictable
name and bone, house
to trap the self: this self
pinned to *Eve*, obedient
aspect of the oblivion.
I heard a music then, the first
laughter lingering in the sylph-like clouds

as though it were the language of light.
Alabaster and mother of pearl
layered the east, territory of that know-it-all
Lilith, hardheaded in her patina of dawn.
I never saw her
though her sound was all around us,
and she did have a being
if not a collarbone. And no fret
in her, no scorch or broomstraw,
all my soon-to-be accoutrements.
She would go on hovering in the distance,
monochromatic, a liminal
reminder, almost imagined
as I rose out of sleep—a leitmotif
to accompany me:

the risk of God's perfection.
In me, the arbitrary
spirit of dirt, changing form
and arriving unexpected
as the silverfish born in clean dishes.
That silt I held tight in my palm
rubbed into the skin to show
an ambivalent lifeline.

Some gesture shook me, like falling
on the edge of sleep—a shudder
passing through my limbs.
Nothing opened but my eyes
full of sand and salt,
then the mouth, its tongue
tasting. I bit the fat of my lips.
I wanted to know
whatever mass I had come to,
I wanted a mirror . . .

And I don't mean words,
those tacked-on shadows,

blindnesses. His names
sprang up like mushrooms overnight,
parentless in the wet air. Tiny
sculptures of spores—those syllables
lay everywhere. With the art of dust
they blanketed every living thing.
Names to cover South, the dark red oxen,
cane, guava and indigo.
North with its cows, their udders
dragging, fuschia and potatoes.
The real being beat like a pulse
beneath layers, a moth
caught in curtains, an invisible
thumping in the hollow of a tree.

Voice was what I learned
in spite of naming. Utterance
in the hum and croak, all the discrete
utterances for being. Pig squeal, the whistle's
low liquid sky. Song was my narcotic,
full in my mouth, the rising O
from my tropical center. Voice broke in me
smooth as dove, ragged as a banshee. The riot
of the good crow. With it I forgot
who I was. Give me a few new sets of feathers
and I'm a bird of paradise, singing to strut
after the permissible fruit:
cloves, nutmegs and the brown anise flowers.

2. Other

He descends in a rainbow of cobalt and mauve,
ambiguous as water. Lying over that sigh
of beauty and rage, God creates Adam: a bone
crossed by six ribs, his swelling.
Out of heaven's dust, the worm
already mingled with man. It's that diving into earth
God wants, not the eel crossing the surfaces of sea.
And if its body is made from the body
of Adam's leg, God means that leg as tree
rooted to one place, as the other will want
always to carry him away
on feet which are the boniest of fish.
God knows feet are too visible,
more clumsy than fins. His own legs glide
under petals, part veil, part skin.
God needs no muscle, he is two arms and a face,
he's one gorgeous pair of wings.
The lover, with his outstretched hand—
he opens the flower of Adam's face and sees himself
in the one he gives breath. God is blind with wonder
and regret. He pulls away with every stroke
though he will not bear the distance.
This love will be God's undoing. This is the denial
even before Eve, that consolation and sweet
invention of play. This is the first
terrible longing, and in God's rapt gaze
the tearing away.

3. The Invention of Need

In the whole of his body not a grain of salt,
born as he was of pure clay and the firmament's
blessed water. Destined to walk
with his face in the clouds, he hardly saw me,
though I was his lens, the question
in his inventory. He'd examine
some bird's flight, never seeing
I was the branch from which it flew.
If he was the foot, I the intricate
mesh of bones; part of him
yet unknowable, a separate
source of thought: muse and therefore
the mystery he was tied to, inescapable
joy or dread. When we walked, he listed
toward me; the animals put their mouths to my palm
and the trees leaned. Something in him
swayed . . .
              If I was his first craving
then I was his guilt. He knew God
watched somewhere. All the purple things
were blooming by the water.
We walked among the clear tiny irises
and the bunches of lilac hung down. All ours
but without necessity,
like the lion and deer in their muted furs, standing
solid around us, all props
in that pretty theatre of blame.
Like a parent, Satan watched from the side;
he floated, wingless, skinny
in the face of what we had. We saw
the sky's river, we saw its bed.
I wanted the fish of Adam's hands,
fish of the current
spawning, green with names.

4. The First Dream

In my sleep, I woke
to devils fighting. The cross-weave of tree
shadow hung down over me: a woman
lay dead at my feet. I saw a world
inexplicably male and made of refusal.
I knew Adam would be lost to me.

Then I turned to the leaves
for the chatter of those tongues: such profusion
to blanket the red fruit—
even in Eden nothing matched it.
Adam cultivated prayer and a hunger
for testimony, giving every other tree
its name. Adam was a leaf himself
in the wind of God's beating.
Over me the one tree

opened like a lover. My hesitation
shifted like the shade. In all things that shine,
apple skin and eye, I saw my face
reflected as I would have seen
a stranger's. I lay there
enclosed in the tree's one season,
waiting for change

in that wood of self-murderers.
No knowledge in paradise
except in the manifold
fruit of God's tree.
The taste was of the self:
it said possibility. It allowed
my hand on Adam's cheek. He ate and saw me
and we joined. We left the garden
as one leaves childhood and its blind
sufficiency. We left
for the risk of other, that love
we know in the few moments
shielded from loss.

5.

The geometry of the fall: me,
the snake, the tree. First the leaves
flew away, as if to make more birds,
later our sign for a winter coming.
But the branches doubled
their forbidden fruit
and made thorns, thorned sky
above the trunk, thorn of snake
bite and lightning
studded the sky. Around us
all melody ceased, no movement
in the arbor but the snake's
branch and flicker,
no lengthening of the fig.
Then light, a light
rose up and his split tongue
began as if the earth were speaking.

That bed of rock and fossil
held the root of wanting. Over it
the tree, the fruit—so much red
hanging, like the gaping of his mouth.
I saw the path his tail made
to the cover in the reeds.
Come to me, little mother of desire.
Taste the sugar of this fire, it's another
color of love I'll show you.

Nothing resisted.
I held his head, my mouth
held the apple in his mouth.
I stood on the spiny root
of the tree, the snake and I
one starred curve against the trunk.
That tail was another language
wrapped around me. God knows
you are the secret, it said,
and so I found the globe

in his mouth, the world of knowable things.
And for the first time, Adam turned
away, to the sky's angular thrust
as if he could not see me, beginning then
a turning which has never ceased. Poor man,

love was then betrayal
to the god who henceforth
would be locked inside him.
I gave him what I could,
kisses and fruit. I sewed our skins.
We were deep in flesh
and earth. Our feet sank
into the ditch that was our path
out of there.
And always below us, the snake's
tunnel of fire.

6.

We slept as lovers and claimed our Eden.
I thought we claimed the dark as well—
merely an absence of light,
like the body's sweet black places.
But when we turned from each other, cold
cracked the porcelain sky, the ocean
lay bound by ice, and frozen in that water
without nerve or light, the dead surface of our names.
Caught by the hook and merge of obligation,
Adam resumed his naming. In my body's eye
child-light gleamed, the giving up of ease
for a self-made grace that would not heal
the fracture. God's thunder
broke my reflection in Adam's eyes:
in that joining, the paraphrase of our lives.

7.

Blind in a pit. The black wing
of the body let loose.
What is the soul but a line
to hold, held by a sail
full in the wind. You, falling
through knowing and not knowing.
A wire catches. The spider dangles,
instructed by the weaving,
the gift. And still you hang.
It is what we call *lost*,
the certainty of falling,
as when you come to the edge of sleep
and something jerks you back.
You are trying to wake yourself,
trying to hold on,
needing to be saved.

8. News

God screeched: pine and frenzy,
hawk shuddering. The yew tree spiraled
closed to pray, and one answer
tore it down. Nests flew
through the furious leaves, thorns
grew up on all the simple grasses.
The steel blade of his wind
slashed through the sea's bowl
and the water gave up its glass.

The bottom of the land
rose out of the sea, islands
toppling, the world sliding, every atom
rearranged. Kill
found its hoot and moan, lightning
split the hills. What did not burn,
drowned; in God's tantrum
the birth of weather—nature's
undertaking to save itself.

The rain drove us out.
The incoherent black
whipped the rivers around us,
laid hold of the gut and squeezed,
cramp by cramp until our own bodies
revolted and gave up all speech
for a vile liquid erupting.
All of God's poison made water: it poured
on us and out of us, tearing every earth
in the avalanche of our dismissal.

God wanted gamble and choice, his own distance
established for us all: mine from Adam,
as Adam's from the worm curled inside me.
God made him an iron boat called faith
and floated us away.

9.

O the whirligig of God, the ice wind
of his dancing, his trillion angels on a pin.
He's caught in the flight of my hair,
tangle and yank. Love, love, love,
he says, God's rhapsody. He's
blowing kisses in a cyclone;
now he stings and now he smiles,
wire in the blood, bite in the side
of the inevitable apple. I'd forget him
if I could, but he's riding the weather.
He loves to throw his light around,
his wing, his million gratuities . . .

When he says forgive, it means
blow on the cut place;
where we find nest after nest
of the most delicate wings,
he lays a swamp.
And wherever a precious stone
all the rock he can build over it.
He's loyal to the clay's rigid vein,
spits in the water to make it salt.
He claims anything I put a hand to:
the little green I coax
out of the stubborn dirt
and every ounce of my weight.
He's the clang of the soul
shutting its gate.

10.

Give a kiss to the goddess of smile and spit.
I've got everything evil to discover—
the first sweet spy
born in a veritable minefield.
First the borrowed rib, then the real body
under skins, draped in the original
classical manner: dishabille and the resulting
sluthood of clothes and temptation.
I'm the queen of night, the music of black,
crusader for the seal's cry or beached
whale, guarding the generic fear
in the crack of the oyster and piss clam
banged on the rocks. Crack of the helpless,
that's my province.
                              And the paralyzing need:
give it up and you'll give up
the religion of the Fall—and me,
drafted for what I'd bear, God's gift
to Adam, promoted and diminished.
Here comes the sour mother of the usual
entreaties; the keeper of pain,
emotional juice in the vein, the blossoming
bruise of the morning-after
invisibility and Adam's
inevitable shrug. What to do but cope.
It's what I'm best at, the politics of coping:
plow and suck, book and bottle
into the twenty-first century.

THIS WORLD

1. Adam

Eden didn't build my heart.
No desert there, no stone I've learned
to rest on. I stumble through
swamp bite, the sea in its fit, all for naming
snake and the trick of snake, the worm
in the sand, too many waters. Nothing severs me
from skylight: he sees to the cursory slash.
I keep to the words, I'm slave
to his endless families of creation.
I, the father of names, and she
little mother of hungers.
We make a household, this sulking
cocoon of two minds and the shape it takes
between us: the *no* we suck. All for the love
we were cut for, that hell of interpretation
won't shut up, remembering all the old
paths to paradise. She's full of want,
one nervous wing that can't fly us back.

I'm tired. Hush to heart, I say, hush to the old
mercurial non-dance,
swelled vein in the wrist, the bound
thud of it. Hush to God, all the requirements
for doubt and grace. Earth's the occasion:
I eat its dirt and thistle.
I make it the iron in my throat,
I make it speak.

2.

All histories are fabulous;
ours stinks with genius.

3.

Because of her, sorrow
to men who eat bread; because of her
I'm fixed between a double kingdom.
She can pierce a bird's heart
with a long straight pin: I pin the name
Queen Alexandra's Birdwing
on that lovely thing
folded in the leaves. Who can say
what we're made of? I can believe
the backbone is a handful of small stones

stringing us upright in the morning,
saving in us a kind of spring—
when comes some blossoming,
when comes some little keeping
and its place for the shortlived
iris, the more durable lily.
Untrustworthy as May
spring comes, a little chance
for perfection, and so I open
to the intensities of body. Every pore
is a threshold to the senses:
the eyes and full lips,
the flower of the face

she holds briefly up to mine.
There's the expectancy of rain in her,
her silence like a flock of crows,
wary as a shoal of mackerel. To want
is to not want, is the tide's
movement toward and away,
like the sheen of silk falling
from her body, the play

of her mouth on mine,
rousing what word, what fire
in my throat. She wants to hear it.

But I'm overcome
by the taste of her, nipple to mound.

This part of herself she can afford
to give up. Put your weight on me
she says, and I shudder,
recoiling as if my finger had touched
a bird's eye, or the opposite:
a wall collapsing over me.
When I look at her then

I see some germ, some density,
an infusion. Something in me
craves her mockery as it craves water,
or my release in her. Afterward
nothing's sayable. It's fear, I think,

of that jungle of names: *Lilith*,
Laylah, in all of them
another translation of night.
The riddle in the wine, the stripper's
masquerade under the cover
of darkness. Willful
goddess of the nocturnal emission,
succubus, demon, attacker of the sleeping . . .

Here's the theme: order against love.
For just a few seconds, give in
to the body's atomic disorder, the come
in the throbbing I and thou,
energy pulled from fire on water.
This desire is a burning shard of glass;
black smoke, this female and male.
And everything in me wants to keep her
from the ancient wind she was,
sweeping and pressing
my every crevice, clinging and letting go.

The lie of her calm,
the layers: death and grace

in her wild hair, like a shine
igniting straw. Sometimes I think
God's brittle order
shattered when he ignored
the genesis of her name.

4.

This world claims every color
in its catalog of grief.
Blood of the poppy
opening for the yellow
filament, the defiant
eye of the pansy,
where too much red goes purple,
goes black. Fist and chin:
points for the bruise of being,
skin rasp on the elbow
I hold myself up with. The rose
mapped on her body, the pinks
revealed and hidden, and I go after them:
nipple, tongue, lip.
Teethmarks on skin, the indented blue.
The fading red under the scab,
the raised white scar.

It was not a question of need.
She came out of nothing but a bone
from my side. Rib of no-pain,
rib of the ideal, the intended
bridge, the faulty connection.
The rib for caution, the flimsy bone,
weak without its many brothers.
But made of body, after all, with the lovely
curve of contradiction. Pain's
predecessor, the original
bone of contention.

                    First thing I saw
was my blood on it, the same I see
working this parched land. The blood
of repetition, before the callus.
Red to her means one month,
the wet she wakes to;
means beet or berry,

fuschia and variety.
Red for what's alive or dead,
the chicken's neck in her hand.
She shrugs off the name, all surface.
As I would shrug off what I'm made of,
hatred or shame, words I've made
in the trap of her thighs, her pale side
punctuated by the row of faint blue lines,
the cage that keeps me
from whatever god escaped me
in the one bone. I'm limited

to the open and close of my hand.
Knuckled and veined, the hand of failure
ordering time, framing
silence, bringing me back
to the razor and noose of this world
flying up in front of me;
the flinch of my body
wanting what my eye can't stand.

5.

She says naming
keeps me from the thing, serves my need
to blame, an assignation
of distance I'll maintain
at any cost. My sin
is self-sufficiency, but she's got
the easy proverbs. She calls
the night *lyric*, she makes the killer hawk
dance on the warm carnage of its kill.
As if seeing were a game,
she's with the sheep
flocking down to the lake. I look,
with my plain language.
Where's the rhapsody in the waves?
Some commotion tarnishes the water
just so—the waves spinning. The circles
fly out and collide,
enough to warn me away.

Because all of earth seduces,
lust pulling me in. What's the rib
but polite talk. He yanked it out of me,
all the tenacity of body
born in that motion.
When I look at her, sometimes an anger
surfaces in the name of love,
as if those small shoulders make in me
a union of resist.
The way I lug the field, cursing it
free of stones, the kick in me
for all the backbreaking ground
it's my job to convince.
All this in the small of being.

So I do penance with this flesh—
washing with broken ice. I make myself ice,
rivaling the stars I count
until they are like the stones I haul away,

the ones I lift above my head
courting tension, just to fight the edge
of giving way.
            And the earth rings
with what I have to say. I hit it
with everything I've got, holding nothing back
but breath, until the being of no-breath
tightens its rope around my chest.
Like running hard to be empty. It's this
pain I pay with, the currency
of dominion over desire.

6.

She's the flute my breath forces.
She does the singing.
It's the same with the wheat's
gold stream lifting
before the harvest, before the drying
forces it to straw
and I bind and stack it, that beauty
foreign to me as the black well
that gives me water, as the fragrant
tunnel under bedclothes,
where I know her
as the hollow taking my shape.
She carries what's alien
inside her: the gleaned bone, my seed
growing until the human
thrashes out. No virginity
in how she's made. Her whole being
means connection. She gives birth
like the moon eating the black sky.
She's got my envy
in her full belly, she's got the child
for sacristan and totem.

7.

God keeps to his heaven. He burns,
seeing. I burn to see,
marked by a blaze I can't get to
in spite of earthworks:
the infant in the cradleboard
or the absolute and inviolable
beauty of flowers. What use
did he have for them,
owning as he does the whole of light?

And he's busy with it—
throwing purple on crimson,
the colors of yell and scream.
He burns up joy and sorrow
like straw in an east wind. He made me
for his eye, his gleam
in the whole of black, a weight
to make the bodied word.

8.

So we who had owned the earth
became its sharecropper and beggar.
We learned what the seed could do
and what it would refuse.
Wheat was our discipline,
not the fruits and flowers we took,
such examples of paradise
in the face of exile. We brought them
out of earth to bury again,
to lose our longing for loveliness,
to see it break. We were children
with our curses, brutal to the ox we needed
to plow, to grind
the kernel of the stiff gold weed.
Brutal in our desires—
to see them break.

LESSONS

1. An Introduction

Steel yourself, I cried and fought the wall.
Two of me now, one on either side:
the one who administers
while the other screams. It's another hemisphere
where I've crossed over, pain
at the north of it, pain at the south.
And all of it in the fiery hands
of God or no God—what matters?
No earth can hear me
through this acre of white fire,
the burn and the burn
in the yanking forth of some new creature,
something to redeem us. Redeemer,
what's that but the solid absence
when the pain stops, like a rope held out
to a secret door I can't reach before the splitting
tears at my gut again. That fist
claws me down and down
until this is where I live:
in the birth of mother, in the push and shove
of cruelty and love.

Push and I am exiled
to the push of the homeless, the blind
burning ball inside the push of the planet
pushing through the great black space.
What's inside here but a world
ripping me apart; what's to be born
but the effigy of this world's
frantic coming undone.

Dullness nursed by quiet, and I come back
to something like a gull's wing, an inexplicable
opening in the sky and I remember
the dawn. In that small time, a hand
is delivered, then arm and shoulder
and then the whole of the baby man.

2. Words, As If They Were Air

To be born is to hear your mother's voice screaming,
to drag out with you her living red gut
like an animal split open.
To be born is to be severed and shaken,
naked in hands and watered with tears.
I know there is a heaven—I've cried at its gate,
torn from the child, and with the child
a self torn away.
Wholeness is heaven, we will not enter there.

And the miracle of exquisite pain
is how the memory fades
like the bruise under my breast
where the foot at nine months kicked inside me,
blue-black along the ribs.

★

Words go through me
as if they were air, a wind
that never stops shifting.
I understand what I can't put my hand through:
the tree's rough width,
the rock in the dirt.
Inside the earth, husk after husk
buried or burned. A certain wood
whistles in the fire, a finite music
like the bird in my mouth
or whatever translates
the wingspan of my arms. What they hold
defines the hour. I can find
two weeks in the anemones
that whiten the field, three days
will break an iris. Summer's time
nests in the hedge, winter's home in the root,
as my earth has its season
for taking the seed. The baby grows
to complete the body and to leave it.
What's to keep when we say *mother*?

Someday they will dig up the far pasture
and know the word in that nest of bones
resting between the bones of her pelvis.

3. Grain

What we love will shatter us.
I plow, I fight the hills
for the chemistry of change,
the chemistry of grain, that currency
of currencies. I trade my life in it,
tornado and earthquake of it, the fat stream
billowing. It's a natural calamity
and I'm buried alive.
Wheat: the seed-swollen grass,
fifty spikes to a plant, a hundred grains a spike.
Specie after specie, we live for it.
Wheat under the pillow of the threatened child,
wheat for the barren; sixty-two
different kinds for the Greeks.
Hunger-bread, from drought and disease
and acid soil, from the hard-nosed God
who thinks to teach me a thing or two.
His color again: stem rust
replacing green and gold. Generation
to generation, dwarfed or too tall,
savaged by black. All of them:
Turkey Red, Rent-payer, the earthy seeds
of drought-resistant winter wheat
and the hard red spring. We're after
the tonic husk of bran, the germ—
fighting army worms, witchweed and the red-billed
Weaverbird with the home-brew
of boiled sorghum and cattle blood.
Make a life out of it:
woman pounding the indigestible hull,
man lacing tall stalks for fences.
We'll burn the entrails of a sheep,
burn a red dog, believe Satan owns it
in sow thistle or wild oats.
There's barley for the fat of it,
cakes for the enemy, for the carp and livestock,
for the beer.

You want prayer? Pray for deliverance
from the rusts, the most dazzling
of earth's proliferations, and the Hessian fly
sucking the juices, collapsing the stalks.
Pray to the God of the barberry bush,
the maker of these things,
the maker of our stumbling onto this ground.
The rye he contaminates with damp weather—
eating it we foam and burn: St. Anthony's fire
afflicting the thousands who know
the witchcraft of wheat,
who throw themselves in the river to drown.

Brown or white, it is what we break and bless;
it's the smell of the earth in our breaths,
another rib we break our backs for.
Millet and the inferior sorghum
for strength, for the arid soil,
the water we don't have. The harder,
the darker, the better for us.
I swear I'll break it with an ax.

But it takes a cool hand to breed plants.
Drifting pollen against the spike and floret,
anther and pistil: trying to get right
what one good wind can blow away.
This is the good sex, this one
fuels the right hunger. Like accuracy
in the right word. I talk to them
and the plants answer, the sound-stirred
beards of wheat rubbing on each other.

Forget what's underneath.
Cultivated soil is humus, is mold:
dirt, shit, peat, stone. Burned bones,
shredded rose, toenails and wire.

Droppings, old nests, silver paper
and bits of string. Newsprint, all the various
seeds, eggs and turds that make stone.
This earth is one big belly
of stink and possibility.

It's easy to see the woman in the wheat,
her hair like a pale heap of it,
changing color in time, going brittle.
She aims her right foot forward,
using her body for prayer
when she puts in the seed.
I go forward with some words
against ruin, and when I go home
I enter the fragrant air of her baking.
One loaf has all the feminine virtue of the wheat.
I take in her bread, and the woman
takes me in, felicity
in the slender gold of one long strand,
like whiplash in the shape of snake
moving across the field.
In the Eden of no-hunger,
wheat was made for wind, not blight.
Now the one symbol for a hungry man
has a hundred names: Calcutta, Red Fife,
Ethiopian Pride. You think it's not a business?
Wheat for the lottery, the bid,
the saving, the bank and warehouse,
the recipe, the woman who will bury me.

4.

What we love will shatter us.
When I lie down
the weeds appear, the wheat
withers. The morning after
I ache to my core,
the body's anarchy
overthrowing what I am taught
to govern. I lie down flat,
picking clean between rows,
flat for the small of my back
or in water to take the itch.
Didn't he promise
this toil, everything dual?
Oil and water from my forehead,
the blades of my shoulders;
from the infant's greasy meconium
to the black of my bowels.
Add that to the light
of the eyes, open and shut,
seminal and dying.

Two-thirds of my heart consumed.
The other share is mine
but what word
can fight the plow,
charting the calendar of feelings
against the field's metric lines.
If we break the bread and dip it
in the blood of the lamb,
the bleating on the hill
still matters. As when someone
half wishes harm, so asks
after what he knows you love:
how is your little girl now, is she well?
and those words settle
between you and what you cherish,
until it seems the child is in a dark place

with night coming on, and you are desperate
to find her.

I try to make a song
out of what needs saying.
I never get it right, though once or twice
a word rises unbidden
and flies with a kind of lilt,
that careless bob a bird can make
in mid air. Or the weaver's ease,
those colored yarns
ordered before the shape begins.
The nearest to happiness
is that moment of its leaving:
at dusk the light's loom
stringing the sky. And the river
so still it means nothing
but the ribbon of its name . . .

Not like these babies
always beginning
to walk and speak, a world
too fast in flux
completing and completing.
The infant face in pimiento
under the jaw, the strongest bone
in the finished body.
O little marrow
of what we are,
swift currents . . .

5. Three Losses

The little one already sleeps with a word.
Tucked alongside her in the brass bed,
I find the bright felt markers,
their colors on her face and hands.
Not even five, she's ready:
write me a note, she says, and put it here
to remind me not to put pens in my bed
I find her lying on her stuffed horse, a pillow
larger than she is, watching the moon.
She is quieter than sleep
in the inaccessible hours of the night,
willing to leave me undisturbed
by her private life of need,
though something in the moon has always
troubled her. *Noise*, she first called that light
burying her baby face in my neck.
It's what she holds on to that she knows.

★

With the next child
the rattle in the doctor's instrument
said *murmur*, the vital beat
caught up on a rocky shore,
that wall of a heart where a hole
had been pounded. We listened for the practical
thump of the fetus, that movement
like a speech which guarantees
a universe. To have a child waiting
means listening in the night
for the calculated rhythm of the planet.

★

There was one I understood;
lily-weight she was, too white.
I could hold her in the palm of one hand.
When I found her, throat locked
against the air, I forced my own
into her like a storm,

until her eyes opened to the nothingness
behind them and the pounding
in the drum of her flesh
fell away.

Would she have been the one
to name it all outright? To say it exact,
without the warp and weft—for her
the cut of accuracy.

6. Sons

We find him dead.
That moment like a rock thrown down
on any voice or reason. What god
is responsible, what lives?
In all our dark assignments, never this
stable of hatreds:
two brothers and the necessary god
on the roof of belief, another snake
in this test of hoe and shovel.
All his life, that one bent
steady over the ground; his look
turned in me like black earth
turned to take the seed.
Sheep followed the other
as he moved through the fields
hardly seeing. Gazing with his endless offering
he was his father's child.

I woke that morning asking
why the water had locked still
over the underworld of fishes;
why in the field the grasses lay
crossed over and stiff.
A minor reproduction of Eden
found the repetitive
glass of the lake, two swans
poised in the lapidary light,
as if carved on a headstone and our world
were its grave.

★

Grief distorted Cain's face,
a grief that would cross the sacrificial ages,
Abraham in his thicket, and beyond.
And almost acquiescent,
that emptiness in the victim's face, that homage
paid with the ram's
lovely antique head. Cain's eyes

went to black glass, the knife
bone-tight on the haft, as if to arrest himself
before that silver broke the air;
as if some hovering dream
had played back brother, *played back*
murder, *and the deed could still be*
wrestled out of him in the sweat of a nightmare.

Abel's arms were raised as if to embrace Cain,
his eyes sleepy
and blameless as jeweled stones
offered to the Lord: the male god
of giving and taking back,
the worship or destroy.

Cain leaned into his brother's body like a lover summoned,
moving into him as they must have moved together in the womb.
He drew the blade up under the ribs as easily
as child's play, and they sank to the red-furrowed dirt;
Abel's hands resting on his brother
as if in benediction.

★

Adam stood speechless at the son who ran,
his face reflecting all the complication
of judgment and heart.
I fell on the body
I could not heal with all the medicine of hands.
When I finally walked away
there rose in me such a coldness and formality
that I would never wholly join
the world of simply being.
All words became a great teasing
and sleep went to live outside me—
all things physical
opened my eyes: no moon but a cradle,
no cradle but face.

Rain came in long sheets,
making silver out of blood, silvering the knife
with shimmering beads of ice.
The new green bobbins of the apples
clattered to the ground, the body
shining like the great underside of a fish.
He lay there and the world continued.
How many brothers to make a genocide?

7.

I know this place; it's made of wire
strung tight, every ligament of the jaw
straining. Wire of contusion,
circle of white teeth, of the moon's
outline, copper and acid.
Wire of the fist, the ankle, the shove.

Anger is the true speech,
made of ridicule and contempt.
Is that what this world's about?
Some sweet pride, then,
decays inside. Oh this
nagging tooth, a rot lost
deep in the nerve. A garden fermenting.
And yet the flower: the iris of the face
gleaming through the blackness
of the frame. The face you have fixed
as the one true thing.

*

Grief becomes the place
I go for blood and ashes. Until now,
the words held—a basket
in which all sense rested, babies
my seed brought to being. I made
two sons. Death is what I gave them,
my eye fixed on the heavenly sky.

Take care of this moment
above all others:
this one already leaving
but separate from the great vocabulary
of the past, of pain.
Rest the moment of this word
in the dead brother—no longer a man
but the sound my mouth shapes
to bring back the one who answered to it.
A sound that lives

to compose sorrow, to call him
back into my body. He lives there,
the ache and tear of a word
as it enters and re-enters.
Listen now; listen.

8.

I wake with a debt. I surface
with the taste of blood, iron
in my mouth. Years of waking
to something wrong—the same dream
you can't remember—and the temporary
emptiness when no words fill your head.
There's a name just out of reach,
important because it escapes us,
quivering in the air, held like a raw egg
unbroken in your mouth.
I'd like to live like the hangman
with just one thing to say: to ask
forgiveness of the damned.
I'd give up this inventory of sound,
this tone and wit I don't have, the flat howl
of wind talk, the rattle of screens,
every speech-building music.

My whole posture is made of words.
I am no more than the tensile filament
of my breath which bears the name,
the canticle and web—the slit throat,
the testicles, every word
dowsing the body for relevance,
naming the hand's argument.

Language: pay close attention
and you'll lobotomize the senses.
The old concierge comes
dressed in black, keys at her belt.
What can she remember
except the wider and wider road
of betrayal, stepping out of language,
out of detail, as if to guard against
a certain suffocation.

In the anarchy of all my words
only one speaks revolution.

Eve makes the litany,
the bee in my ear, the racket,
the avalanche, the quake.
You can hear her in the vanity
of my speech; she colors the black and white,
makes knots in the thread, endless
insomnia of words. She's my fever,
intoxication, the music I can't shake
out of my loneliness. She says
we speak in order to come closer.
The truth is, we like to hear ourselves:
our inaccuracy.

I'm talking about a dictionary of misunderstandings.
Every word stakes out its own
territory. The word as hermit, as clan.
The ones in pairs: the easy *love* and *betrayal*.
Wrong and *satisfy* to catch your ear, the poetry
in *sensation* and *flux*. To get it right
means the pulsing of an artery, a raised eyebrow,
means to plug into the circuits
of sun and moon. I want the kind of talk
that makes porcelain, where the conditions
have to be hard. I want the one right word,

though I'll search the several meanings,
like pruning the trees for fatter fruit,
like the equinoxes of December and June.
All the opposites show you for a fool.
And the words like *obsidian*
reach out and go on reaching: the river's lie,
a silk scarf over the knotted current;
the night storm—obsessive, the explicable black.
A word dragging its history behind it,
the word as tool, to avoid a crisis or to deny.
I wear them like the halo of my misfortune.
In words, my visible character:
my stutter, my vertigo, a longing to fall.

9.

So many rains and the years
unmeasured. Same hunger, same thirst.
Wheat, locust, flood: all given to words,
while back and forth, the moon
nailed its course, seasons fell and the infinite
pieces of light. And what held vigil
over my shut door? My own little mercies,
native keepers of warm,
my snow and wool—all of earth's blankets
under your tin histories. O my governors,
tell me what is real; find me a lifetime
in which I am not used:

the midwife of your nightmares. My job
to pull that chaos out of you, so you can
dream an order, a comfort
in the leashed tides, my periodic flow.
In all of earth, this is the message:
divine but unclean.

Look into my hand.
What hasn't it dug?
What path won't cross this web of lines,
the ribs of the fingers,
the basket of bones? Its sins
are of the moment: callus and ache,
the fish it let slip
as the fin sliced its way through,
my own running blood, and lost too,
the baby's month-old foot.
This hand will fall to rest, go free
in water; make a cup and hold fast
the nipple and child, the dark red plums
and the worm and slug
in the mouth of the ground.
The seed it planted
is reborn in the fruit—
two hands to gather and split it,

as two hands make a knife
for the tearing of meat.
One hand to coax, but two hands
beseeching or rising in anger,
to clench and shake
or take by the throat—the fist
releasing the palm that rests
all night on the pale burning head of the sick.

★

I know a world unsayable: beyond Adam's
harvest or the bread I make from it,
beyond the composition of any given body.
Walk in the woods, after rain, in heat
and there will come such a rising up,
such richness in the heart of dark and dirt,
that the very rise and fall of your chest
says *earth*, says *be*.

Multiply knowledge and you
multiply desire: the meat of the apple.
The shock of entering, fear
bearing down on the muscle,
and the pulse two bodies sustain.
The sound of breath in pleasure
is the sound of breath in pain.
Out of the blind hours of birth,
hurt gives way to the love of child,
and for that little time, we are
saved and remarkable.

For in all pain, the passion.
The germ tears the kernel
in the opening of the seed. Out of paradise
we ate the passion of the ground.

★

I've come to know
fullness, the unexpected,
as in my breasts when the milk let down,
or when that moment of sky
slides over the sun.
And from one tree a flock of birds
rushes like a great fan
closing on the rain-fat land.
To remember is to belong.
Ordinary water holds the dome of the sky.

10. Earth

You see a woman of a certain age,
not old, yet seeing every sign
of how the world will age her.
More and more, you'll find her in the garden
but not for onions or potatoes.
She wants blooms, color,
a breaking in the earth's disorder.
Swollen branch, the right bird—
they can make her cry. And the fussing
over moving this or that to the right location.
Learning to be alone,
she brings out ten varieties of rose,
armed against pest and blight
and the cutting northern cold
she fights with blankets of dirt.
Earliest spring will find her hovering
over the waxy perfection of tulips, the ones
closest to the thawing ground.
You'd think it's the opening she loves,
the loosening flower revealing
the meticulous still-life deep in the cup.
But what she needs is to see
those stiff-petaled, utterly still ones
rise out of the dirt.

The weather won't cooperate. She sinks
hundreds of bulbs in the rain,
mud on her hands, black smear on her neck.
For this birthing, all she pays
is stiff joints, and she knows again
the insistence of flowering.
Falling, she knows the flowers
fall to the season, and the seasons
to the great wheel. Fallen, she's learned
to prefer the fallen.

11. The Art of Exile

Hope eternal: what's that
but weather. So much glitter on the water,
those points of knife-light in a million
small shrugs. A light made of indifference,
Eve says, the hook
dragging for the drowned man. But it is our
instruction, and I accept

the longing in the sky's rim
coming up against the black wash.
I've sat through the night to see that color
opening for the rush of light.

So this is separation: a grievance
we never leave, because he chose
to split the void; male
and female held apart, as the sheer
white of the wave crest
builds to break its spine,
as the darkness is a vessel
no light can fill.

★

I cover myself with work.
Nothing endures, not sweat or shudder,
that embroidery on the senses.
You, God, who once laid morning gold on me,
you cover me
with your continual creations:
the neck of a deer, the squirrel's
perfect eye. You've made the world
your justification, your flaw.
Where else can I find your light
except in the gull's beak
biting the water, diving to rise
with something silver in its mouth,
any rubbish made holy by the sea.
These boundaries have everything to do

with failure. I walk out by the water
in which some fierce non-animal
rages, the sea complete unto itself,
like the slug which contains both the sperm and egg
and so has banished all desire.

But you're the loneliness
at the base of my throat, the spittle and sap,
the live self
confined to the trap of my words.
Cackle and mumble, I'm defender
in all the bush leagues of the personal.
You make the limits, confine
the freaks and graces, find the doubter
on the brink of release.
Here I am, praising
the delineation of your every detail.
I walk into the tangled woods and walk out
with *blackthorn, whitethorn, ash.*
The art of exile.

★

In one small patch of grass
so much color. The purples go
both pink and blue, their petals
thick as flesh or paper-thin.
Around them, the long swaying
white and straw-tipped grasses hide
yellow beneath. They make an ornamental trail
to the dogrose bank, the bridegroom of thistles.

I marvel. The earth is indeed beautiful,
without guile and full of increase,
a heavenless place
on water-black ground.
Ignorant of any death
it pulls me in, astounds.

12. Given What Manages

This is for the daughter,
heiress to a fortune in grief, a paradise
and so the loss of one. They made her
heroine of the hurricane: no flattery
to share the female name.
This time she'll get credit,
discovering the eclipse and comet; the romance
hurled to earth, the morning
white in her face, too many kisses
or not enough. By thirty she can't believe
the ugly business of winter: leaf by leaf,
the trees give up everything
to survive. In her own house
crows feet and the widening
network of veins. And this hunger she's got—
an eye for food, the endless
fat or thin, shrink and scold.
Regret for the baby she turned from,
guilt for the one in her lap, how she takes in
the pure air of that little breath.
Destined to be of two minds
she's the heartchip and the nag,
keeper of the sponge,
the bedtime and the bed.
Instead of love, she learns mercy
requires knowledge. She buys herself
a net and a killing jar, and goes out
into the remarkable summer field
(the baby is napping, the ring's on the sink).
Before the summons of that bright yell
she went to the woods, walking to see
the fox and deer. And to repeat the infinite
names from all the books, the regeneration
of wild. Once on her mountain, she discovered
the burrow of the last great rattler, the last poison
that high up in the East.
Fierce for him, she scattered
leaves and brush against the spot,

and hearing human noise, ran
deeper into the trees. As if she were a deer—
then like the deer she could do nothing for,
stumbled finally back to the road.
All through late winter's grip
she walked to find the herds
whose hunger would have forced them
to the bad bark and pencil-thick stems
that rip like cloth the lining of the stomach;
forced them to the crushed and mangled
winter bushes, where to suffer that gnawing
they all lie down.

               Now squinting in the noon buzz
she gathers the easy weeds, some to admire,
some to eat, rubbing off the dirt with spit.
Uncovered in the glare, the clumsy insects
scatter and fall. And what is it inside her
still holds and releases?
She writes in her book: "Given what manages
to survive on this earth, who are we
to think we could know trauma or triumph,"
and sits until sweat
trails down her neck, between her breasts.
She uses the net to jar what's common,
the horsefly and bee. After supper she'll draw
with clarity and precision.
She'll draw them as they have not been.